STEPHEN BIESTY'S
MORE INCREDIBLE
CROSS-SECTIONS

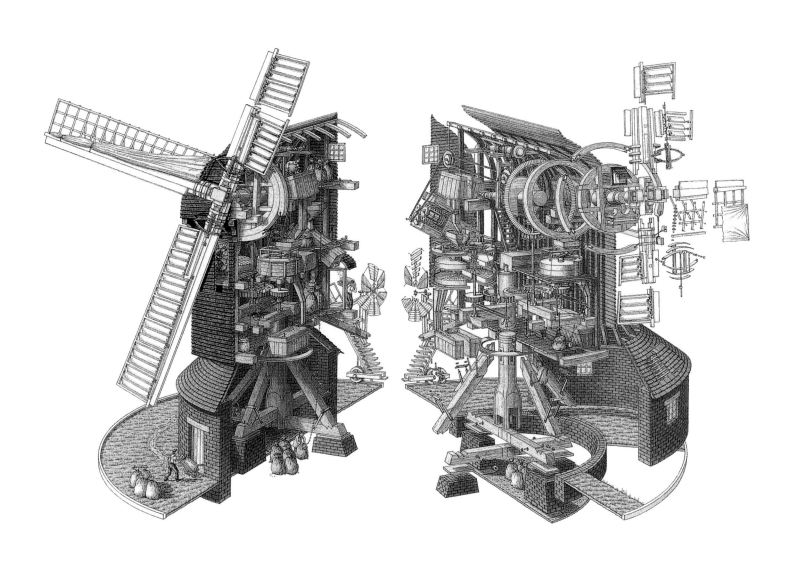

STEPHEN BIESTY'S
MORE INCREDIBLE
CROSS-SECTIONS

ILLUSTRATED BY
STEPHEN BIESTY

WRITTEN BY
RICHARD PLATT

DK | Penguin Random House

Art Editors Dorian Spencer Davies, Sharon Grant
Senior Art Editor C. David Gillingwater **Senior Editor** John C. Miles
Production Louise Barratt

REVISED EDITION
Senior Editor Camilla Hallinan
US Executive Editor Lori Cates Hand
Assistant Editor Andrew Korah **Assistant Art Editor** Srishti Arora
Jacket Designers Akiko Katu, Priyanka Bansal
Jacket Editor Emma Dawson
Jacket Design Development Manager Sophia MTT
DTP Designers Bimlesh Tiwary, Rakesh Kumar
Pre-Production Manager Balwant Singh
Production Manager Pankaj Sharma
Producer, Pre-Production Andy Hilliard **Senior Producer** Jude Crozier
Managing Editors Francesca Baines, Kingshuk Ghoshal
Managing Art Editors Philip Letsu, Govind Mittal
Publisher Andrew Macintyre
Publishing Director Jonathan Metcalf

This American Edition, 2019
First American Edition, 1996
Published in the United States by DK Publishing
1450 Broadway, Suite 801, New York, NY 10018

Copyright © 1996, 2017, 2019 Dorling Kindersley Limited
DK, a Division of Penguin Random House LLC
19 20 21 22 23 10 9 8 7 6 5 4 3 2 1
001–314840–October/2019

A catalog record for this book
is available from the Library of Congress.
ISBN 978-1-4654-8573-1

DK books are available at special discounts when purchased
in bulk for sales promotions, premiums, fund-raising, or educational use.
For details, contact: DK Publishing Special Markets,
1450 Broadway, Suite 801, New York, NY 10018
SpecialSales@dk.com

Printed and bound in China

A WORLD OF IDEAS:
SEE ALL THERE IS TO KNOW

www.dk.com

Greetings Earthlings!

The atomic drive and date controller on my space cruiser have broken down. Now when I try to land on your planet, I keep crashing at the wrong place and time. This is annoying for me, but it is a great way to meet Earthlings. You have all made me very welcome: artist Stephen Biesty helped me mend my craft when I crashed near his home. I told him of all the other places I had seen, and he drew them for me, so I had a souvenir of my trip to Earth. Perhaps you can spot my landing sites—there is one in each picture in this book.

Reproduced by Dot Gradations, Essex
Printed in Italy by L.E.G.O.

Contents

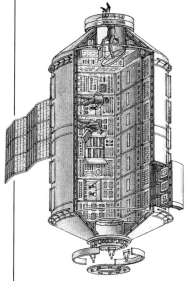
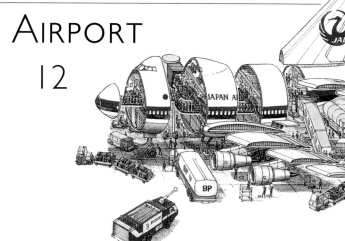

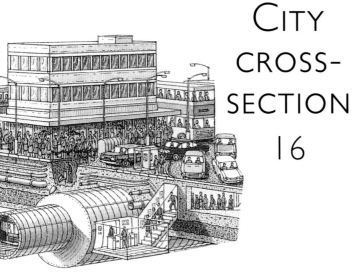
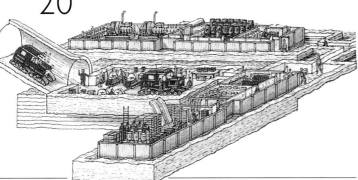
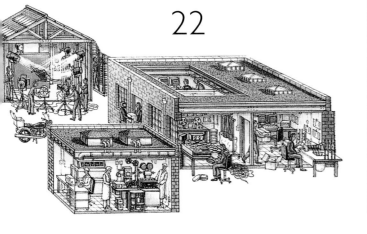

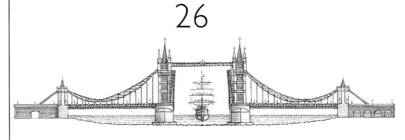

Traction Engine

HISSING, STEAMING, CLANKING, AND SHAKING the ground, traction engines are like mechanical dinosaurs. Almost extinct, they were once the most modern form of power. Traction engines first appeared around 1860. At first they powered stationary farm machinery such as threshers, which separated kernels of grain from their husks. Later engines pulled plows or heavy road wagons, and turned amusement rides. For a while, steam represented a bright, labor-saving future. But the reign of the traction engine was a short one. By the beginning of the 20th century, electric motors and internal combustion engines had begun to take over many of its tasks. Before long, the puffing monsters were making their last journeys—to the junkyard or museum.

On the belt
The engine could drive machinery, such as a threshing machine or a power saw, if a leather drive belt was looped around the flywheel. Often a traction engine would be used for threshing in fall and winter, and as a power saw at other times of the year.

Forced water
Since the boiler is under steam pressure, water must be fed in forcibly with an injector. When the engine was running sweetly, the injector could often be heard "singing" quietly like a whistling kettle as it let jets of water into the boiler.

Steering
All traction engines were self-propelled, but early models required a horse for steering. Harnessed between the shafts of the engine, the nags did not have to work hard.

Creating steam
Heat to boil the steam comes from burning coal in the firebox. The stoker continually feeds the fire to keep up a good supply of hot gases. Hot gases from the firebox flow through tubes inside the boiler, making them so hot they boil the water, creating steam. The gases then flow from the boiler tubes into the smoke box. From here, waste heat and sparks are blown out through the chimney.

What the steam does
Steam from the boiler flows up around the cylinder into the valve chest. A sliding valve lets steam shoot through the valve chest into the cylinder, pushing the piston forward. The valve then slides back to let steam in on the other side of the piston and push it backward. As the piston slides backward and forward, it pulls on the connecting rod and forces the crankshaft around. The turning of the crankshaft drives the flywheel.

Spud pan and chain
Steering was never easy on a traction engine. It relied on a hefty chain attached to a large drum between the front wheels, called the spud pan. When the driver turned the steering wheel, the steering bar pulled on chains to turn the wheels.

Governor
The "governor" was a device that regulated the engine speed. It was a valve opened and closed by two spinning metal ball weights. When the weights spun too fast, centrifugal force moved them outward, lifting the valve to let off steam and slow down the engine.

Water jacket
Too much heat could make the boiler blow up. So, apart from the open grate at the bottom, the firebox was entirely encased in a jacket of water.

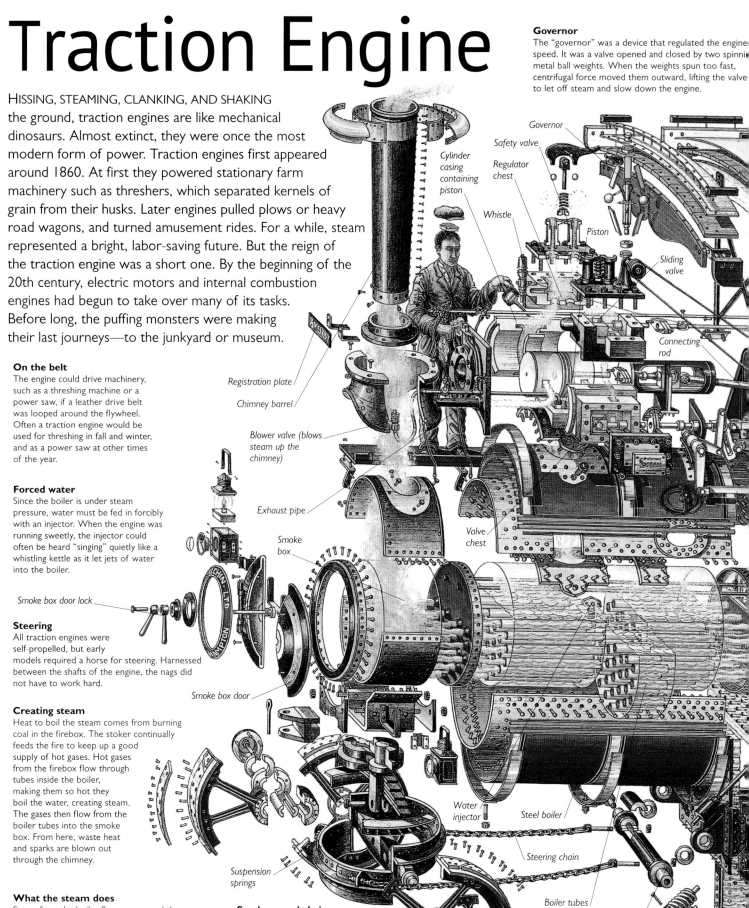

Governor
Safety valve
Regulator chest
Cylinder casing containing piston
Whistle
Piston
Sliding valve
Connecting rod
Registration plate
Chimney barrel
Blower valve (blows steam up the chimney)
Exhaust pipe
Smoke box
Valve chest
Smoke box door lock
Smoke box door
Water injector
Steel boiler
Steering chain
Boiler tubes heat water
Steering bar
Worm gear
Suspension springs

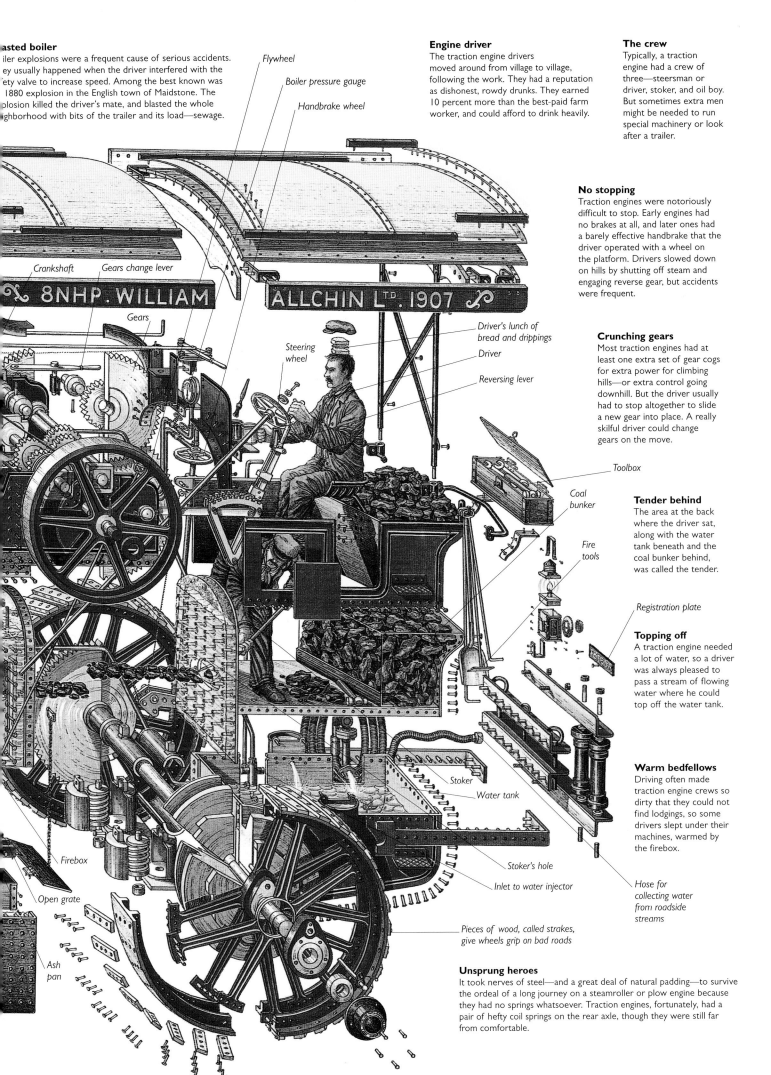

asted boiler
iler explosions were a frequent cause of serious accidents.
ey usually happened when the driver interfered with the
ety valve to increase speed. Among the best known was
1880 explosion in the English town of Maidstone. The
plosion killed the driver's mate, and blasted the whole
ghborhood with bits of the trailer and its load—sewage.

Flywheel

Boiler pressure gauge

Handbrake wheel

Crankshaft *Gears change lever*

8NHP. WILLIAM   ALLCHIN LTD. 1907

Gears

Steering wheel

Driver's lunch of bread and drippings

Driver

Reversing lever

Engine driver
The traction engine drivers
moved around from village to village,
following the work. They had a reputation
as dishonest, rowdy drunks. They earned
10 percent more than the best-paid farm
worker, and could afford to drink heavily.

The crew
Typically, a traction
engine had a crew of
three—steersman or
driver, stoker, and oil boy.
But sometimes extra men
might be needed to run
special machinery or look
after a trailer.

No stopping
Traction engines were notoriously
difficult to stop. Early engines had
no brakes at all, and later ones had
a barely effective handbrake that the
driver operated with a wheel on
the platform. Drivers slowed down
on hills by shutting off steam and
engaging reverse gear, but accidents
were frequent.

Crunching gears
Most traction engines had at
least one extra set of gear cogs
for extra power for climbing
hills—or extra control going
downhill. But the driver usually
had to stop altogether to slide
a new gear into place. A really
skilful driver could change
gears on the move.

Toolbox

Coal bunker

Fire tools

Tender behind
The area at the back
where the driver sat,
along with the water
tank beneath and the
coal bunker behind,
was called the tender.

Registration plate

Topping off
A traction engine needed
a lot of water, so a driver
was always pleased to
pass a stream of flowing
water where he could
top off the water tank.

Warm bedfellows
Driving often made
traction engine crews so
dirty that they could not
find lodgings, so some
drivers slept under their
machines, warmed by
the firebox.

Stoker

Water tank

Firebox

Open grate

Ash pan

Stoker's hole

Inlet to water injector

*Pieces of wood, called strakes,
give wheels grip on bad roads*

*Hose for
collecting water
from roadside
streams*

Unsprung heroes
It took nerves of steel—and a great deal of natural padding—to survive
the ordeal of a long journey on a steamroller or plow engine because
they had no springs whatsoever. Traction engines, fortunately, had a
pair of hefty coil springs on the rear axle, though they were still far
from comfortable.

Fire!

BURNING IN A CITY BLOCK, FIRE IS LIKE A DANGEROUS MONSTER. It attacks your senses one by one. You can often smell the hot-tempered beast before you see it. As a fire grows by consuming everything in its path, you hear it too, first crackling then roaring in your ears. For town dwellers, the fire monster is an old enemy, and one that has never been far away. Today we're learning how to control the monster and curb its appetite. At home, simple safety precautions such as smoke detectors warn of danger. If flames take hold, an emergency call brings brave firefighters rushing to the blaze. Water from their hoses cools the flames, and creates steam that starves the fire of the air it needs to burn.

Don't panic

Recent research suggests that fire rarely causes panic. Though aware of the danger, people usually help each other escape. A stampede to safety happens only when victims believe the fire is about to cut off their escape route.

Anybody in there?

Firefighters must search every room to make sure there's nobody unconscious, asleep, or perhaps too old or ill to move.

Fetching hoses

Elevator shafts in new buildings are protected against fire, so firefighters use them to rush hoses to floors where they are needed.

Bad elevator buttons

Some buttons don't have to be pressed: the heat of your hand calls the elevator. In a fire, they're fatal—the heat calls the elevator to the hot floor.

Wet risers

In most countries, tall buildings must have wet risers—pipes that channel water to hydrants on each floor. Firefighters connect hoses directly to the wet riser.

Chopper rescue

When the tallest buildings catch fire, rescue by helicopter may be the only escape for those trapped on the upper floors.

Alarming facts

Fire alarms should alert everyone in the building to the danger. Nevertheless, experience shows that when there are no other signs of fire, some people don't recognize the alarm signal, or they just prefer to ignore it.

In the dark

In a smoke-filled room, visibility is zero, and firefighters have to navigate by touch alone. As they search, they pay out a cord, so that they can retrace their steps to safety.

Sprinklers at work

By spraying a fire with water, automatic sprinklers can put out flames before they take hold. Room temperatures much higher than 140°F (60°C) fracture a soft metal strip or a tiny glass bulb on the sprinkler nozzle; water then sprays out, covering about 130 sq ft (12 sq m).

Save my pianos!

Automatic sprinklers are not new. Henry S. Parmelee of Connecticut invented them in 1875 to protect his piano factory from fire. New England cotton mills made them a success—the fibers they processed made the mills a big fire risk, and without a sprinkler system, mill owners couldn't get fire insurance.

A long way down

The tallest turntable ladders reach floors up to 165 ft (50 m) above the ground.

Fireboat

When a dockside building bursts into flames, fire authorities can call on the city fireboat to help. It more often sprays water or

Spreading smoke

An elevator shaft can channel choking smoke everywhere. Newer buildings incorporate pressurizing fans that force air into the elevator shaft, keeping it free of smoke.

Helicopter rescues victims

Sprinkler

Aerial ladder

Hydraulic platform

Hydraulic snorkel

Aerial platform rescues people

Smoke rises through ventilating shafts

Fog nozzle sprays wide area

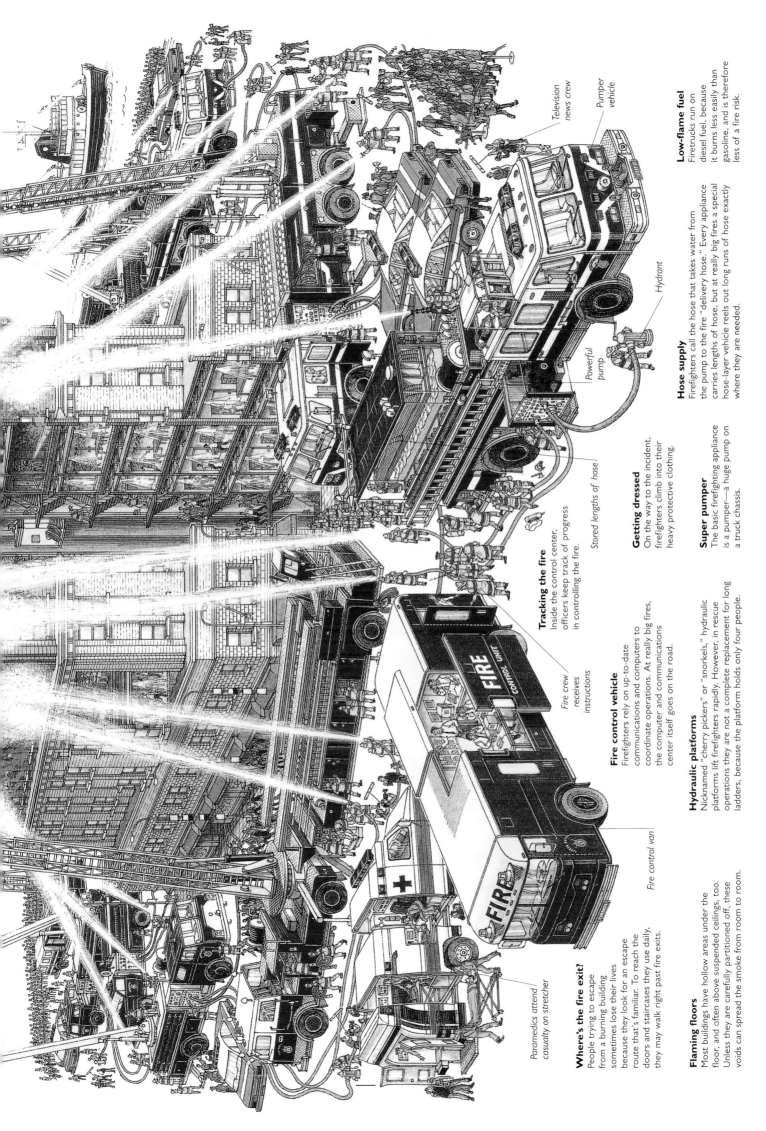

Television news crew

Pumper vehicle

Hydrant

Powerful pump

Stored lengths of hose

Tracking the fire
Inside the control center, officers keep track of progress in controlling the fire.

Fire crew receives instructions

Fire control vehicle
Firefighters rely on up-to-date communications and computers to coordinate operations. At really big fires, the computer and communications center itself goes on the road.

Getting dressed
On the way to the incident, firefighters climb into their heavy protective clothing.

Super pumper
The basic firefighting appliance is a pumper—a huge pump on a truck chassis.

Hydraulic platforms
Nicknamed "cherry pickers" or "snorkels," hydraulic platforms lift firefighters rapidly. However, in rescue operations they are not a complete replacement for long ladders, because the platform holds only four people.

Low-flame fuel
Firetrucks run on diesel fuel, because it burns less easily than gasoline, and is therefore less of a fire risk.

Hose supply
Firefighters call the hose that takes water from the pump to the fire "delivery hose." Every appliance carries lengths of hose, but at really big fires a special hose-layer vehicle reels out long runs of hose exactly where they are needed.

Fire control van

Paramedics attend casualty on stretcher

Where's the fire exit?
People trying to escape from a burning building sometimes lose their lives because they look for an escape route that's familiar. To reach the doors and staircases they use daily, they may walk right past fire exits.

Flaming floors
Most buildings have hollow areas under the floor, and often above suspended ceilings, too. Unless they are carefully partitioned off, these voids can spread the smoke from room to room.

Space station

WHICH WAY IS UP? HERE ON EARTH, THE ANSWER IS EASY. BUT TO AN ASTRONAUT ON BOARD a space station, it's a silly question. "Standing up" or "putting down a book" don't mean very much when everything is weightless. We get a sense of up and down from gravity. Scientists working on space stations call this weightlessness "microgravity." They can use it to make ultra-pure crystals, or exotic alloys (mixtures) of metals, and to study the way weightlessness affects body chemistry. Microgravity can be a problem, though—walking is difficult when there's no gravity to keep your feet on the "floor." So is drinking if the coffee floats around. Spending months in space also weakens bone and muscle, so regular exercise is a must. The International Space Station currently orbiting Earth has been continuously crewed since 2000, and may eventually be replaced by an even larger "orbiting village" like the one shown here.

Satellite capture
One of the main uses of the space station is the repair of damaged satellites. The crew uses the remote manipulator arm to capture the satellite, or to transfer it from a remotely operated robot that collects the satellite from a distant orbit.

Spaceplane
To travel between the space station and Earth, future crews may use a spaceplane. Looking like a small Space Shuttle, it rides into space on top of a rocket, and then flies back to Earth like a glider.

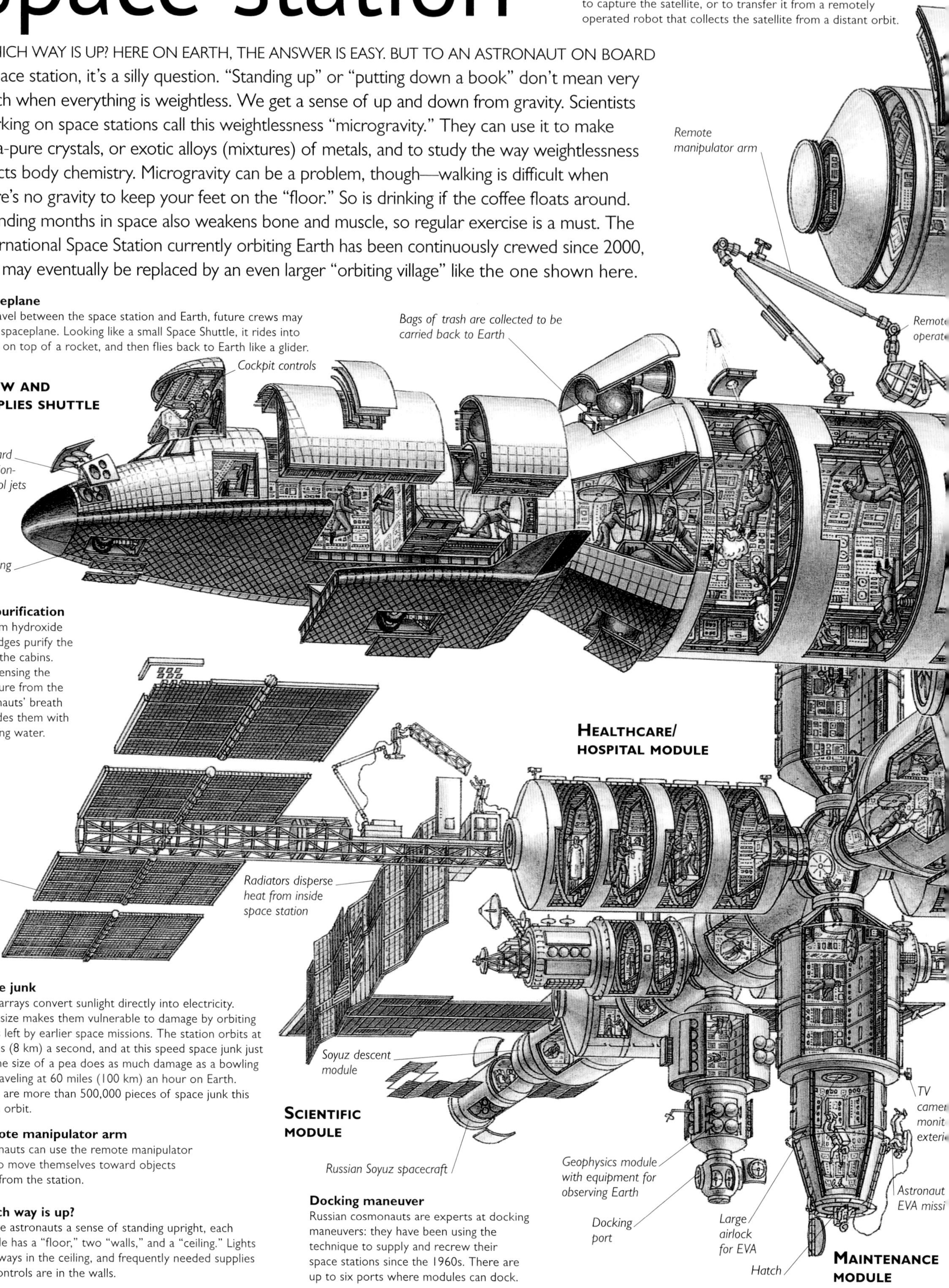

Remote manipulator arm

Bags of trash are collected to be carried back to Earth

Remote operate

CREW AND SUPPLIES SHUTTLE

Cockpit controls

Forward reaction-control jets

Landing gear

Air purification
Lithium hydroxide cartridges purify the air in the cabins. Condensing the moisture from the astronauts' breath provides them with drinking water.

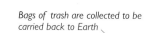

HEALTHCARE/ HOSPITAL MODULE

Solar array

Radiators disperse heat from inside space station

Space junk
Solar arrays convert sunlight directly into electricity. Their size makes them vulnerable to damage by orbiting debris left by earlier space missions. The station orbits at 5 miles (8 km) a second, and at this speed space junk just half the size of a pea does as much damage as a bowling ball traveling at 60 miles (100 km) an hour on Earth. There are more than 500,000 pieces of space junk this size in orbit.

Remote manipulator arm
Astronauts can use the remote manipulator arm to move themselves toward objects away from the station.

Which way is up?
To give astronauts a sense of standing upright, each module has a "floor," two "walls," and a "ceiling." Lights are always in the ceiling, and frequently needed supplies and controls are in the walls.

Soyuz descent module

SCIENTIFIC MODULE

Russian Soyuz spacecraft

Docking maneuver
Russian cosmonauts are experts at docking maneuvers: they have been using the technique to supply and recrew their space stations since the 1960s. There are up to six ports where modules can dock.

Geophysics module with equipment for observing Earth

Docking port

Large airlock for EVA

Hatch

TV camera monit exterio

Astronaut EVA missi

MAINTENANCE MODULE

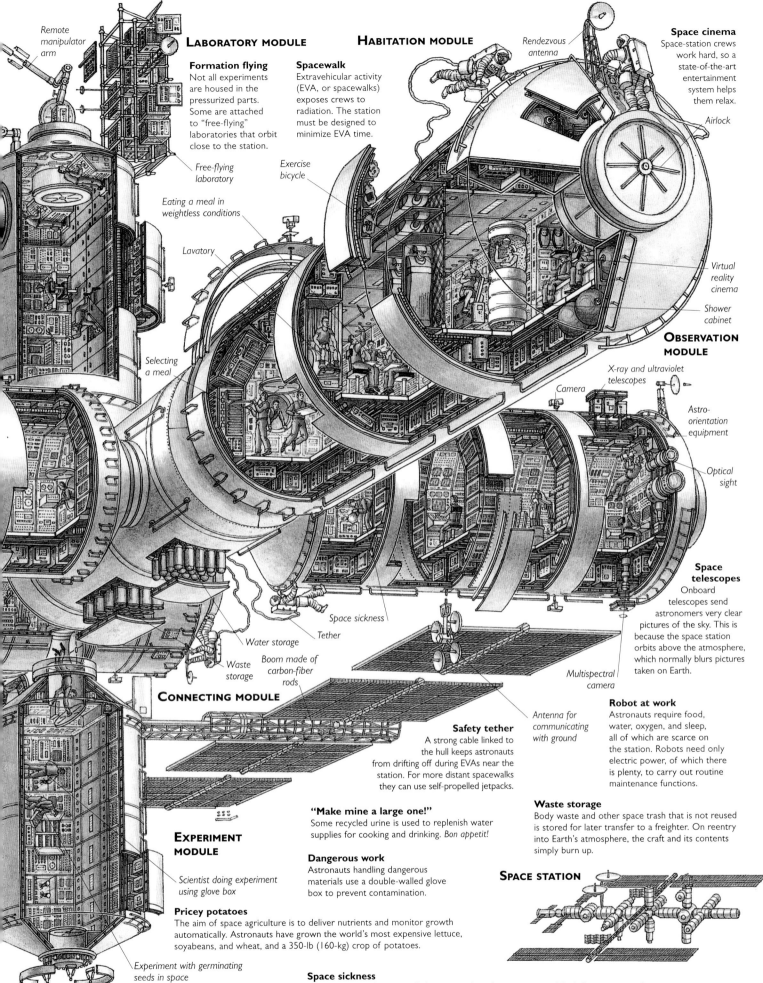

Remote manipulator arm

LABORATORY MODULE

HABITATION MODULE

Rendezvous antenna

Space cinema
Space-station crews work hard, so a state-of-the-art entertainment system helps them relax.

Formation flying
Not all experiments are housed in the pressurized parts. Some are attached to "free-flying" laboratories that orbit close to the station.

Spacewalk
Extravehicular activity (EVA, or spacewalks) exposes crews to radiation. The station must be designed to minimize EVA time.

Airlock

Free-flying laboratory

Exercise bicycle

Eating a meal in weightless conditions

Virtual reality cinema

Lavatory

Shower cabinet

OBSERVATION MODULE

Selecting a meal

X-ray and ultraviolet telescopes

Camera

Astro-orientation equipment

Optical sight

Space telescopes
Onboard telescopes send astronomers very clear pictures of the sky. This is because the space station orbits above the atmosphere, which normally blurs pictures taken on Earth.

Space sickness

Tether

Water storage

Waste storage

Boom made of carbon-fiber rods

Multispectral camera

CONNECTING MODULE

Antenna for communicating with ground

Robot at work
Astronauts require food, water, oxygen, and sleep, all of which are scarce on the station. Robots need only electric power, of which there is plenty, to carry out routine maintenance functions.

Safety tether
A strong cable linked to the hull keeps astronauts from drifting off during EVAs near the station. For more distant spacewalks they can use self-propelled jetpacks.

"Make mine a large one!"
Some recycled urine is used to replenish water supplies for cooking and drinking. *Bon appetit!*

Waste storage
Body waste and other space trash that is not reused is stored for later transfer to a freighter. On reentry into Earth's atmosphere, the craft and its contents simply burn up.

EXPERIMENT MODULE

Dangerous work
Astronauts handling dangerous materials use a double-walled glove box to prevent contamination.

Scientist doing experiment using glove box

SPACE STATION

Pricey potatoes
The aim of space agriculture is to deliver nutrients and monitor growth automatically. Astronauts have grown the world's most expensive lettuce, soyabeans, and wheat, and a 350-lb (160-kg) crop of potatoes.

Experiment with germinating seeds in space

Space sickness
Even before the first space flights, it was clear that some astronauts would suffer from motion sickness (their training aircraft was nicknamed the "Vomit Comet"). Scientists don't yet know why some crew suffer from space nausea while others escape it.

Crystal garden
One of the main aims of the space station is to grow protein crystals in microgravity (near weightless) conditions.

Exploded docking port

Modular construction
An important feature of the space station is its modular construction. Each pressurized section is built of similar units, so that if one fails, it can be sealed off to keep the others safe.

Airport

IF FLYING WAS AS CHAOTIC AS DRIVING, AIR TRAVEL would soon cease. The sky would be black with tiny aircraft. Midair collisions would be so common that newspapers wouldn't report them. At popular destinations, planes would wait for the lights to change, revving their engines and hooting. Then they would race to see who was first down the runway. Of course, it wouldn't work. Flying is just too complex for each of us to own a plane. So at the airport we give up the privacy of our cars. We trust our luggage to a stranger and share the journey with others. Perhaps if we did the same on the roads, our world would be a safer, more peaceful, and more pleasant place.

A souvenir, perhaps?
If you thought the business of airports was transport, you'd be wrong. Commercial operations, including gift shops, bars, and restaurants, bring in up to 60 percent of an airport's income.

Check in
Many passengers are now able to check themselves in for their flights on their own computers and phones, but airlines still offer a bag drop and manual check-in with airline staff at a counter.

Multistory parking garage

Elevator to parking levels

Parking garage and road access

Large airports
Big airports sprawl over huge areas, so "people movers" are needed for passengers transferring between flights. The Dallas/Fort Worth airport spans an area more than 27 sq miles (69.6 sq km), which is larger than all of Manhattan!

Air traffic control
The job of air traffic control is to route aircraft safely to their destination. To do this, controllers must make sure aircraft never come too close to one another in flight, or when taking off and landing.

Tracking on radar
Aircraft monitored by the approach control facility are tracked on radar screens.

Nice view
Aircraft within 8 km (5 miles) of the airport are under the control of staff in the visual control room.

Computer center

Keeping the skies safe
The approach control facility monitors aircraft beyond the circle handled by the visual control room.

Visual control

Air traffic control

Approach control facility

Terminal 1st Floor (Departures) green flow

Bags of space
On average, every 10 passengers on international flights have 13 pieces of checked luggage.

Search me
Scans and searches stop would-be hijackers from carrying weapons onto planes, and electronic scanning can screen checked bags for bombs.

Underground access road

Counting cars
Airport parking areas have to be huge. Los Angeles airport has more than 10,000 spaces, and if all the cars left at once, they'd form a line nearly 28 miles (45 km) long.

Underground railway train

Parking bill
As anybody who has driven to an airport knows, parking is a great moneymaker. It provides up to a sixth of the airport's profits.

Passenger check-in

Take the train
Rapid transportation systems linking national airports to the capital are popular with passengers: half of the passengers to London's Gatwick airport take the train.

Baggage claim carousel

Customs inspection area

Not so rapid access
The belts carrying luggage are like a miniature railroad complex within the terminal: Frankfurt, Germany's, airport has 25 miles (40 km) of track.

Automatic chaos
Computers help plan air traffic, but often controllers keep a manual system, in case of breakdown. They write details of each flight on strips of cardboard and shuffle them into a sequence of landing and takeoff slots.

Runway
The tarmac strip on which aircraft land is called the runway. Its length depends on the type of aircraft using it and the altitude and climate of the airport.

Runway markings
Pilots use painted markings to judge their approach by day in good weather. A standard pattern of stripes marks the center line and boundaries, and helps pilots judge their altitude.

Green for go
A green bar marks the threshold—the start of the runway.

Runway

Smoother than a baby's bottom
The runway surface is carefully maintained to keep it as smooth as a newly surfaced road.

Gliding in
At night, colored lights warn the pilot if the approach is too high or low.

Approach lights
A standard pattern of lights visible only from the air points the way to the runway.

Observation platform for public

Runway may need to be 4 ft (1.2 m) thick to support the weight of the heaviest aircraft.

Main radar

Noise annoys
Aircraft noise is intolerable for people living nearby. A recent study showed that heart disease increased by 18 percent in these people.

Apron

Radar echo
The rotating dish of the main radar transmits a radio signal that bounces back from the aircraft. The reflections show up as blips on the air traffic controllers' screens.

Towing tractor
Powerful "tugs" pull the aircraft out onto the taxiway.

Apron
On the apron (paved area in front of the terminal) staff service the aircraft. They must work quickly because aircraft only make money when they're flying.

Power hungry
Aircraft engines generate electricity, but the supply stops when the engines do. A portable generator then supplies power.

Unloading baggage

Terminal ground floor (arrivals) red flow

Sorting it out
Luggage on the conveyor belt is sometimes hand sorted, but some airports have an automatic system that reads flight numbers from barcodes on tags. The system pushes the bags off the main belt into "branch lines" that lead to the right aircraft.

You're welcome!
The most welcoming airport is on the island of Curaçao. Two-thirds of the people visiting the airport go there to welcome friends or family, or to say farewell. The least welcoming airport is Paris—only 7 percent of visitors are greeters and senders.

Baggage on cart

Crash tender

Smelly rescue
Firefighters are ready for everything. One major European airport is near a sewage treatment plant, and rescue teams are equipped with an inflatable boat and hovercraft, in case a plane overshoots the runway and lands in a sludge pond.

Fill 'er up!
Many airports have hydrants that pump aviation fuel from huge reservoirs. London's Heathrow airport has a store of 14.8 million gallons (56 million liters).

Fuel tanker

Ground crew services engine

Line of baggage
A typical 747 carried 800 pieces of checked baggage. Laid side-by-side, the suitcases would stretch six times the length of the aircraft.

Get a move on!
Baggage from an arriving plane can be waiting on the carousels within 12 minutes, but some airlines take five times as long.

14

Windmill

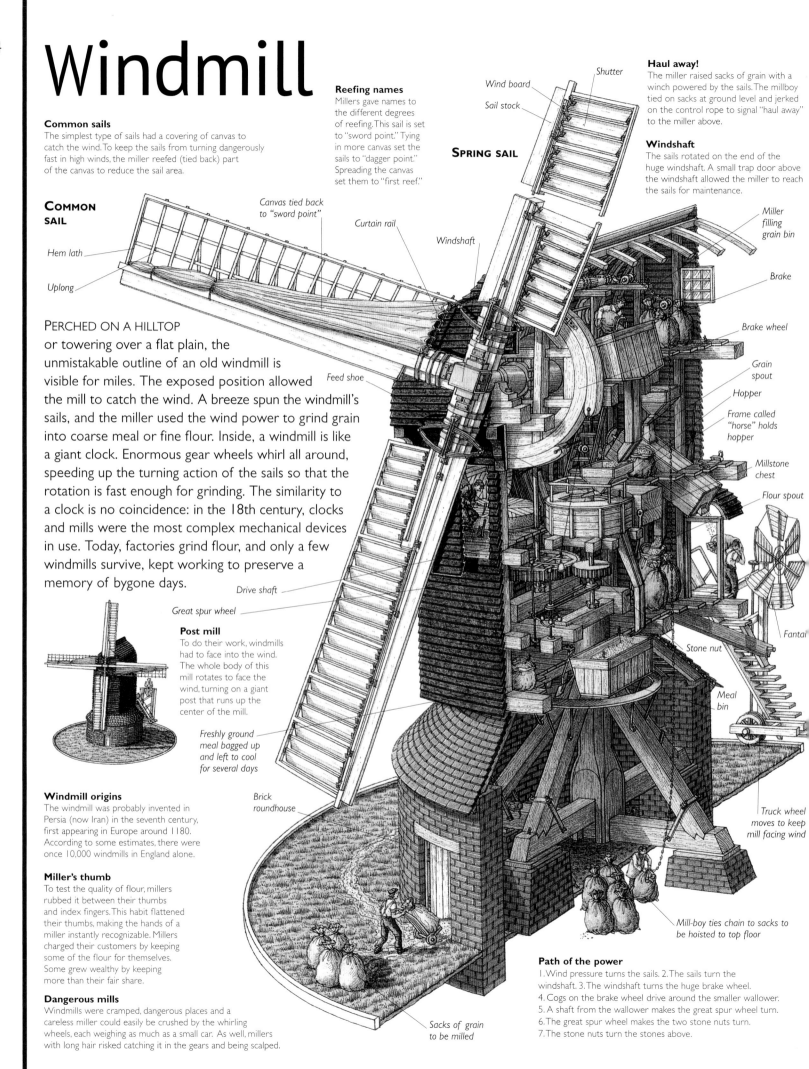

Common sails
The simplest type of sails had a covering of canvas to catch the wind. To keep the sails from turning dangerously fast in high winds, the miller reefed (tied back) part of the canvas to reduce the sail area.

COMMON SAIL

Hem lath

Uplong

Reefing names
Millers gave names to the different degrees of reefing. This sail is set to "sword point." Tying in more canvas set the sails to "dagger point." Spreading the canvas set them to "first reef."

Canvas tied back to "sword point"

Curtain rail

Windshaft

SPRING SAIL

Wind board

Sail stock

Shutter

Haul away!
The miller raised sacks of grain with a winch powered by the sails. The millboy tied on sacks at ground level and jerked on the control rope to signal "haul away" to the miller above.

Windshaft
The sails rotated on the end of the huge windshaft. A small trap door above the windshaft allowed the miller to reach the sails for maintenance.

Miller filling grain bin

Brake

Brake wheel

Grain spout

Hopper

Frame called "horse" holds hopper

Millstone chest

Flour spout

Feed shoe

PERCHED ON A HILLTOP or towering over a flat plain, the unmistakable outline of an old windmill is visible for miles. The exposed position allowed the mill to catch the wind. A breeze spun the windmill's sails, and the miller used the wind power to grind grain into coarse meal or fine flour. Inside, a windmill is like a giant clock. Enormous gear wheels whirl all around, speeding up the turning action of the sails so that the rotation is fast enough for grinding. The similarity to a clock is no coincidence: in the 18th century, clocks and mills were the most complex mechanical devices in use. Today, factories grind flour, and only a few windmills survive, kept working to preserve a memory of bygone days.

Drive shaft

Great spur wheel

Post mill
To do their work, windmills had to face into the wind. The whole body of this mill rotates to face the wind, turning on a giant post that runs up the center of the mill.

Freshly ground meal bagged up and left to cool for several days

Fantail

Stone nut

Meal bin

Truck wheel moves to keep mill facing wind

Brick roundhouse

Windmill origins
The windmill was probably invented in Persia (now Iran) in the seventh century, first appearing in Europe around 1180. According to some estimates, there were once 10,000 windmills in England alone.

Miller's thumb
To test the quality of flour, millers rubbed it between their thumbs and index fingers. This habit flattened their thumbs, making the hands of a miller instantly recognizable. Millers charged their customers by keeping some of the flour for themselves. Some grew wealthy by keeping more than their fair share.

Dangerous mills
Windmills were cramped, dangerous places and a careless miller could easily be crushed by the whirling wheels, each weighing as much as a small car. As well, millers with long hair risked catching it in the gears and being scalped.

Sacks of grain to be milled

Mill-boy ties chain to sacks to be hoisted to top floor

Path of the power
1. Wind pressure turns the sails. 2. The sails turn the windshaft. 3. The windshaft turns the huge brake wheel.
4. Cogs on the brake wheel drive around the smaller wallower.
5. A shaft from the wallower makes the great spur wheel turn.
6. The great spur wheel makes the two stone nuts turn.
7. The stone nuts turn the stones above.

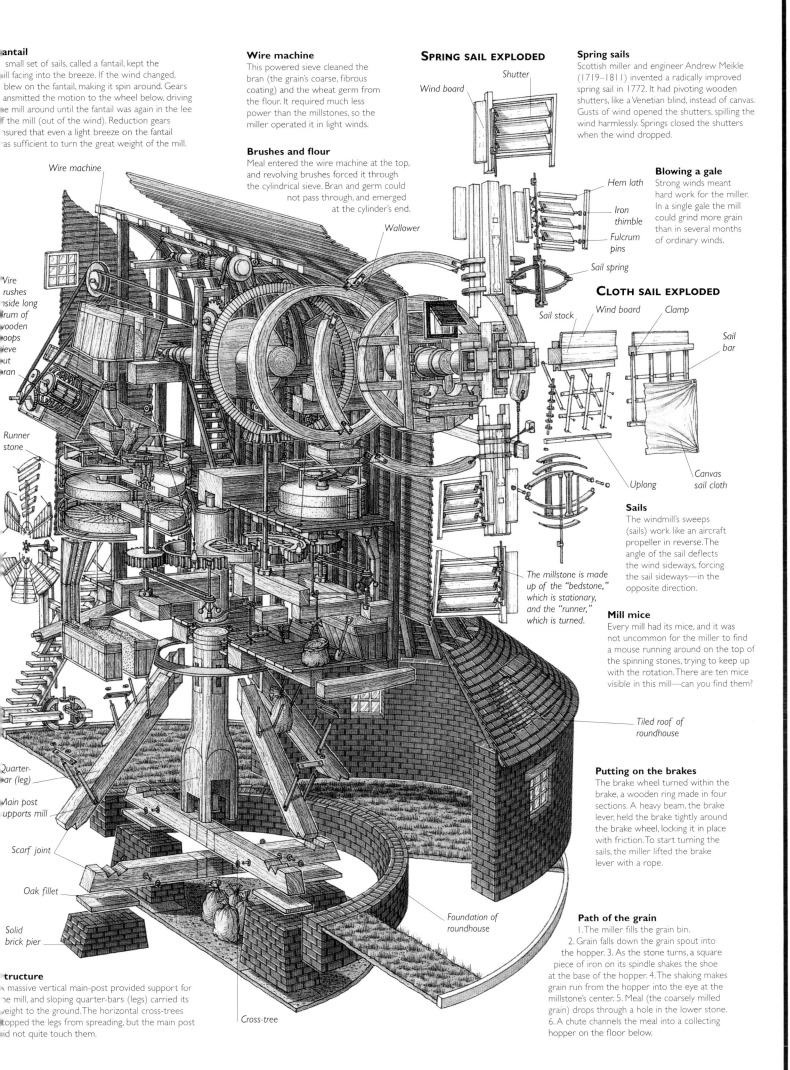

Fantail
A small set of sails, called a fantail, kept the mill facing into the breeze. If the wind changed, it blew on the fantail, making it spin around. Gears transmitted the motion to the wheel below, driving the mill around until the fantail was again in the lee of the mill (out of the wind). Reduction gears ensured that even a light breeze on the fantail was sufficient to turn the great weight of the mill.

Wire machine

Wire machine
This powered sieve cleaned the bran (the grain's coarse, fibrous coating) and the wheat germ from the flour. It required much less power than the millstones, so the miller operated it in light winds.

Brushes and flour
Meal entered the wire machine at the top, and revolving brushes forced it through the cylindrical sieve. Bran and germ could not pass through, and emerged at the cylinder's end.

Wallower

SPRING SAIL EXPLODED
Shutter

Wind board

Spring sails
Scottish miller and engineer Andrew Meikle (1719–1811) invented a radically improved spring sail in 1772. It had pivoting wooden shutters, like a Venetian blind, instead of canvas. Gusts of wind opened the shutters, spilling the wind harmlessly. Springs closed the shutters when the wind dropped.

Blowing a gale
Strong winds meant hard work for the miller. In a single gale the mill could grind more grain than in several months of ordinary winds.

Hem lath

Iron thimble

Fulcrum pins

Sail spring

CLOTH SAIL EXPLODED
Sail stock *Wind board* *Clamp*

Sail bar

Uplong

Canvas sail cloth

Sails
The windmill's sweeps (sails) work like an aircraft propeller in reverse. The angle of the sail deflects the wind sideways, forcing the sail sideways—in the opposite direction.

Mill mice
Every mill had its mice, and it was not uncommon for the miller to find a mouse running around on the top of the spinning stones, trying to keep up with the rotation. There are ten mice visible in this mill—can you find them?

The millstone is made up of the "bedstone," which is stationary, and the "runner," which is turned.

Wire brushes inside long drum of wooden hoops sieve out bran

Runner stone

Tiled roof of roundhouse

Putting on the brakes
The brake wheel turned within the brake, a wooden ring made in four sections. A heavy beam, the brake lever, held the brake tightly around the brake wheel, locking it in place with friction. To start turning the sails, the miller lifted the brake lever with a rope.

Quarter-bar (leg)

Main post supports mill

Scarf joint

Oak fillet

Solid brick pier

Foundation of roundhouse

Path of the grain
1. The miller fills the grain bin.
2. Grain falls down the grain spout into the hopper. 3. As the stone turns, a square piece of iron on its spindle shakes the shoe at the base of the hopper. 4. The shaking makes grain run from the hopper into the eye at the millstone's center. 5. Meal (the coarsely milled grain) drops through a hole in the lower stone.
6. A chute channels the meal into a collecting hopper on the floor below.

Structure
A massive vertical main-post provided support for the mill, and sloping quarter-bars (legs) carried its weight to the ground. The horizontal cross-trees stopped the legs from spreading, but the main post did not quite touch them.

Cross-tree

Antarctic base

IN THE MOST ISOLATED PLACE ON EARTH THE SUN NEVER SETS IN SUMMER—AND WINTER IS ONE long night. The climate is so hostile that no plant or animal can survive for long in the open. This place is the South Pole. It lies at the heart of Antarctica, a vast, ice-covered continent. Antarctica was largely unexplored until seventy years ago. Today, scientists line up to work at this cold and remote south polar base. Why? Because astronomers can peer at the stars for months on end without daytime interrupting their work. Biologists gain a super-clean laboratory: Antarctic air is the purest on earth. And even the icecap itself is a remarkable archive. Locked in its layers of compressed snow is a 150,000-year-old record of Earth's climate.

Polar night
Night begins in March with a twilight that lasts a month. "Morning" comes six months later. In the winter's sky, the stars circle continuously, without rising or setting as they do elsewhere on Earth.

Freewheeling
Tracked vehicles are the main form of transportation at the pole. Coastal bases also use huge-wheeled trucks called Deltas, plus motorcycles and snowmobiles.

Delta vehicle

Tracked vehicle

Weather station

Snowmobile

Explorer's memorial
This drawing is based on the Amundsen-Scott South Pole Station. Roald Amundsen (1872–1928) planted the Norwegian flag at the pole on December 14, 1911. The expedition led by British explorer Robert Scott (1869–1912) reached the pole a month later, but Scott's team perished on the return journey.

Steel arches form tunnel

Fuel storage

Underneath the arches
Steel arches provide much of the indoor space at the base. There shape has been chosen so that the arches shed as much snow as possible.

Garage entrance

The ozone hole
One of the most important jobs of the polar base is to monitor Earth's ozone layer. Each year a hole in the ozone layer opens above Antarctica, and scientists at the base use their instruments to judge how much of a threat this poses.

Supplies storage

Cooking area

Ice on the move
The ice sheet on which the polar station rests is moving slowly. The base moves along with it.

Don't throw water
The low temperatures at the base freeze all water vapour, drying wood buildings until they are like tinder. Fire is thus always a hazard.

Ice movement

Ice moves 33 ft (10 m) per year—the length of three small cars.

Roof arch rests on sides of ice trench

Dormitory area

Work in progress
Maintaining the base demands constant work. Many of the structures are nearing the end of their useful life, and the whole base will need replacing in a few years.

Ancient meteorites (rocks from space) lodged in rock layers beneath ice

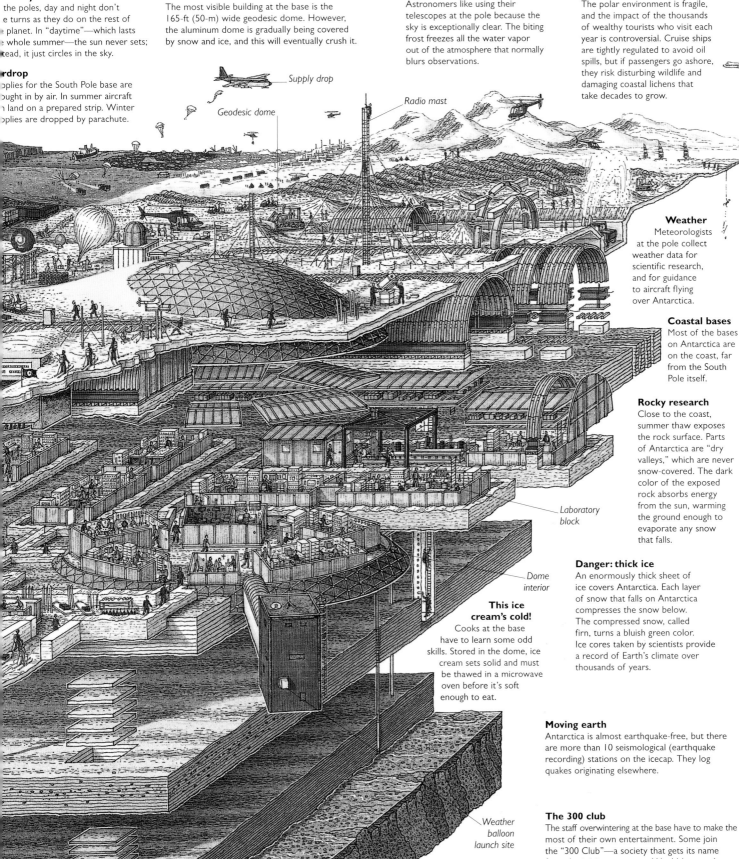

lar day
the poles, day and night don't
e turns as they do on the rest of
planet. In "daytime"—which lasts
whole summer—the sun never sets;
ead, it just circles in the sky.

rdrop
plies for the South Pole base are
ught in by air. In summer aircraft
land on a prepared strip. Winter
plies are dropped by parachute.

Doomed dome
The most visible building at the base is the
165-ft (50-m) wide geodesic dome. However,
the aluminum dome is gradually being covered
by snow and ice, and this will eventually crush it.

Clear skies mean better views
Astronomers like using their
telescopes at the pole because the
sky is exceptionally clear. The biting
frost freezes all the water vapor
out of the atmosphere that normally
blurs observations.

Ecotourism
The polar environment is fragile,
and the impact of the thousands
of wealthy tourists who visit each
year is controversial. Cruise ships
are tightly regulated to avoid oil
spills, but if passengers go ashore,
they risk disturbing wildlife and
damaging coastal lichens that
take decades to grow.

Supply drop

Geodesic dome

Radio mast

Weather
Meteorologists
at the pole collect
weather data for
scientific research,
and for guidance
to aircraft flying
over Antarctica.

Coastal bases
Most of the bases
on Antarctica are
on the coast, far
from the South
Pole itself.

Rocky research
Close to the coast,
summer thaw exposes
the rock surface. Parts
of Antarctica are "dry
valleys," which are never
snow-covered. The dark
color of the exposed
rock absorbs energy
from the sun, warming
the ground enough to
evaporate any snow
that falls.

*Laboratory
block*

Danger: thick ice
An enormously thick sheet of
ice covers Antarctica. Each layer
of snow that falls on Antarctica
compresses the snow below.
The compressed snow, called
firn, turns a bluish green color.
Ice cores taken by scientists provide
a record of Earth's climate over
thousands of years.

*Dome
interior*

**This ice
cream's cold!**
Cooks at the base
have to learn some odd
skills. Stored in the dome, ice
cream sets solid and must
be thawed in a microwave
oven before it's soft
enough to eat.

Moving earth
Antarctica is almost earthquake-free, but there
are more than 10 seismological (earthquake
recording) stations on the icecap. They log
quakes originating elsewhere.

The 300 club
The staff overwintering at the base have to make the
most of their own entertainment. Some join
the "300 Club"—a society that gets its name
from the joining ceremony. Would-be members
run from the sauna into the snow wearing only
shoes, thus experiencing a temperature drop of
300°F (166°C).

*Weather
balloon
launch site*

It's cold here!
Antarctica holds the
record for the coldest
weather anywhere on earth.
In 1983 the temperature at the
Russian *Vostok* base dropped to
−128.6°F (−89.2°C). Mercury thermometers
stop working at −40°F (−40°C), and even alcohol
thermometers can freeze, so meteorologists have
to use special thermometers.

Windy, too
The polar continent is also the world's
windiest place. In some places wind speeds
reach 200 mph (320 km/h), and rarely drop
below 30 mph (48 km/h).

Movie studio

IN THE WORLD OF MOVIES, NOTHING IS QUITE WHAT IT SEEMS. TWENTY to thirty years ago, before computer-generated images (CGI) created all kinds of special effects, movie magic was created by hand. Towering buildings were tiny models. Scary monsters were latex puppets. A space station turned out to be a large sheet of canvas. Making these illusions look convincing required the skills of a huge team of people, including set designers, background painters, and model makers. These specialists crafted the film in a studio complex, working for months on tiny details—only to see it flash by on the screen in a few seconds.

Studio city
The soundstages, where filming takes place, are like huge sheds. They are carefully soundproofed, so that the sensitive microphone[s] don't pick up the noise from traffic and aircraft outside. Though this drawing shows filming taki[ng] place on three sets all at once, normally only on[e] of them would be in use at any time.

The people in the backroom
The sound stage is vast and obvious, but it's only a small fraction of the whole. Clustered round the cavernous set there's a maze of small workshops. Inside them an army of technicians and support staff toil. Without their support the production would sink.

Animatronics
Model makers mold latex foam into elaborate monster masks and screen creatures, such as a small squid. Tiny motors hidden inside the rubber skin control movement of the limbs and facial expressions.

Distant illusion
Carpenters build a quarter-scale replica of the Buddha statue. When it appears in the background it will look like the full-size statue four times farther away. Without such perspective tricks, the studio would need to be four times as big.

Roof structure

Lighting rigs on all sides of soundstage

Buddha model remains unfinished where camera will not see it

Camera crew

Huge boulder ready to roll down the set

Architecture of sound stage

Enormous, heavily soundproofed door

Arm of huge Buddha taken inside for assembly on set

Making small model of Buddha in carpenter's workshop

Model of squid

Film vault

Processing film for editing

Editor/ working at editing table

Matching up/ soundtrack and film

Sound mixing on mixing console

Recording/ sound effects

Producing/ the final soundtrack

Mattress for/ stuntmen to land on

Fitting a/ costume i[n] wardrobe

The cutting room
While a lot of film editing today is done digitally (on computers), some editors still use traditional methods to cut and join a cutting print (positive copy) of film shot in the camera. This is used as a guide for cutting the negative from which the final prints are made.

Matching sound and picture
The editor's assistant synchronizes the film and soundtrack, which is recorded on magnetic tape with sprocket holes, just like film. The assistant checks that the "clap" sound at the start of each scene lines up with the film frame showing the clapperboard closing.

Keep the noise down!
Much of the film's soundtrack is recorded after shooting finished. For footsteps, actors walk around on simulated patches of "gravel path" or "autumn leaves." The final sound of the film may consist of thirty or forty tracks mixed together.

building

...ndstages can be vast. The world's biggest is ...riental Movie Metropolis in Qingdao, China covers 107,640 sq ft (10,000 sq m). That's ...e enough to park two jumbo jets inside.

Speedy sprayguns

Painted backdrops were often used because they were so cheap and quick to produce. Two painters could take just a few days to conjure up a background the size of a tennis court.

That sinking feeling

Stuntmen replace regular actors for dangerous sequences. The stunts are filmed from a distance and later edited carefully. In the past, stuntmen stood in for women, but laws have made this illegal in the United States. The studio can employ a stuntman in drag only when all available stuntwomen have refused the part.

Rubber crustacean

Like the small squid in the model shop, this giant is a latex model. It's a kind of huge puppet, realistic only on the side that faces the cameras. This doesn't mean it's harmless: the rubber shark in *Jaws* (US 1975, producer William S. Gilmore, Jr.) accidentally sank the ship carrying the cast and crew, sending the camera to the seabed.

Studio city

The biggest studios are vast complexes of buildings sprawling over an area as large as some towns. Universal City in California covers 0.6 sq miles (1.7 sq km), and the studio has its own fire department, zoo, stables, and police department.

Wet weekend

To simulate rivers, lakes, and oceans, set builders create huge, water-filled tanks. In 1929, a disused German airship hangar was filled with water to make a 2,000-ft (600-m) long tank that represented Russia's Volga River.

Stirring up a storm

To simulate a hurricane, movie makers attach an aircraft propeller to a powerful electric motor. Besides a convincing storm, the large fan creates a lot of noise, so a realistic soundtrack must be added later.

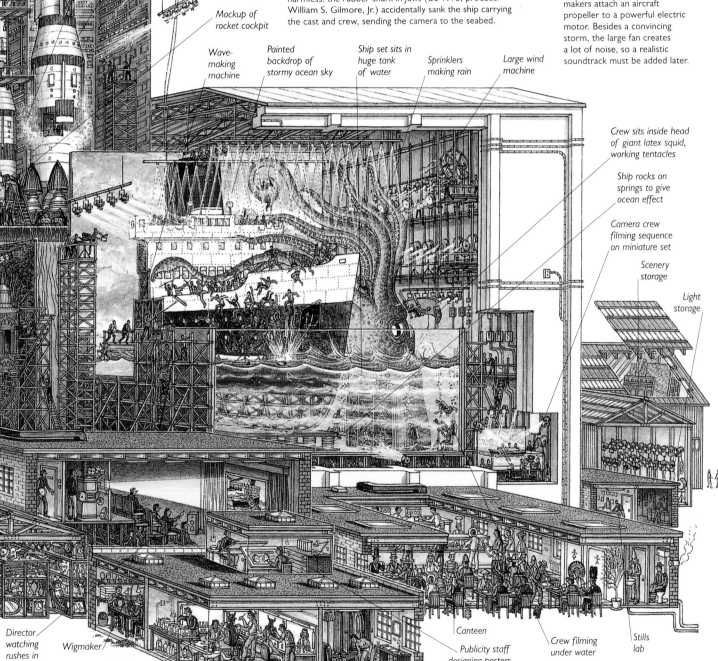

Dry ice inside rocket for blastoff effect

Huge rocket model for Sci-fi film

Mockup of rocket cockpit

Wave-making machine

Painted backdrop of stormy ocean sky

Ship set sits in huge tank of water

Sprinklers making rain

Large wind machine

Crew sits inside head of giant latex squid, working tentacles

Ship rocks on springs to give ocean effect

Camera crew filming sequence on miniature set

Scenery storage

Light storage

...rops ...torage

Director watching rushes in projection room

Wigmaker

Hairdresser

Heavy makeup (the devil)

Light makeup (stunning beauty)

Dressing room

Canteen

Publicity staff designing posters

Crew filming under water

Stills lab

0,000 centurions' uniforms, please"

...he wardrobe department supplies all the costumes. The ...udience sees major stars in closeup, so the costumes they ...ear must be authentic in every detail. Crowd scenes require ...ge numbers of costumes: on the 1951 movie, *Quo vadis*, the ...ardrobe department kept track of 29,000 outfits.

First look

Each studio has a tiny cinema, or projection room, of its own. There the director views the "rushes"—quick prints of all the scenes shot the previous day.

Camera crew

The camera operator has an assistant, who checks, cleans, and maintains the camera, and focuses the lens. The clapper-loader marks the start and end of each scene by clapping the clapperboard and is responsible for loading the film. The key grip on the movie is responsible for moving the camera.

Venice

IMAGINE A CITY IN THE SEA. HALF SINKING, HALF FLOATING, ITS ROOFS AND GLITTERING towers rise mysteriously from swirling mist. This magic place was Venice in the 17th century. Already 11 centuries old, the city had begun as a mudbank refuge from wars on Italy's mainland. Protected from attack by its shallow lagoon, Venice grew into a great world power. An exclusive club of noblemen led by the Doge (duke) ruled Venice ruthlessly. They became wealthy by controlling overland trade between Asia and Europe. The discovery of a sea route to Asia ended the monopoly in 1488; and despite the centuries of decline that followed, the city's fabulous beauty and legendary art treasures survived almost unchanged. The picture shows the central section of the city.

Doge
The Doge of Venice (left) wore elaborate robes made of costly fabrics. He also wore a pointed golden cap called the *cornu*.

Canals
Instead of streets, Venice is crisscrossed by water-filled canals. The biggest, the Grand Canal, is wide and lined with marble palaces. Others are tiny, and one even goes right underneath a church!

Piazza
St. Mark's Piazza is a vast square, roughly the size of 45 tennis courts. It has always been the center of life in the city.

Help!
"Streets full of water, please advise" cabled Robert Benchley (1889–1945) when he saw the city's thoroughfares. His telegram was a joke, but every visitor must share a little of the American writer's surprise on first glimpsing the Venetian canals.

Campanile
The famous Campanile (bell tower) of St. Mark dominates the skyline. Completed in the 12th century, the tower has been restored several times. In the 15th century, criminals dangled in iron cages from the south side as punishment.

Campanile bells
The five bells of the Campanile all had different meanings. The largest, *Marangona*, rang at the start and end of the day's work. *Nona* sounded at noon; and the smallest, *Maleficio*, signaled an execution.

Venetian symbol
The winged lion was St. Mark's mascot. It appears on buildings all over Venice.

Granary
Large stocks of flour and grain in the warehouses (*Fonteghetto della Farina*) enabled the rulers of Venice to keep down bread prices and avoid food riots.

Mint
At the *Zecca* (Mint), workers struck the gold ducats that were the currency of Venice. The coin kept its constant size and purity for more than 500 years, but eventually became known as the *zecchino*. From this word we get the word "sequin."

Books shelved
Venetians began planning a public library around 1360, but the building to house it was not completed until 1591.

Foundations
The buildings of Venice rest on piles: thousands of timber posts hammered into the clay of the lagoon bed.

Campanile

Rialto bridge

Grand Canal

Though Venice is less than 3 miles (5 km) long, the city's 177 canals total 28 miles (45 km).

Piazza

Granary

Merchant ship brings grain

Mint

Library

Piles are made of Istrian pine: the wood gets harder as it ages.

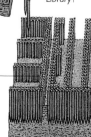

Layout of buildings with canals between them

Bridges
Walking across all the bridges in Venice would be a huge task. There are so many that even guidebooks lose count. The famous Rialto bridge, which spans the Grand Canal, was designed by the architect Andrea Palladio (1508–80).

Venice and visitors
Venice has always been a well-oiled tourist machine, finely tuned to separate visitors from their money as quickly as possible. Even in the 14th century, 500 years before the word "tourist" was first used, the city had inspectors to check travelers' hotels.

Lagoon
Venice sits in a lagoon that separates it from Italy's mainland. In many places the water is only waist deep, but dredged channels allow large ships to reach the shore and to travel out into the Adriatic Sea.

St. Mark's Basilica
Once the private chapel of the Doge's palace, the Basilica is named for St. Mark, one of Jesus Christ's 12 disciples (followers). The *Pala d'Oro* is the Basilica's greatest treasure. This great altar screen is crafted from gold and studded with precious stones. It took 500 years to complete.

St. Mark's

Doge's palace
In the palace, the Doge and his family lived in legendary luxury: the wife of the 24th Doge was said to have bathed in morning dew collected by her servants.

Pala d'Oro

Prison cell

Council chamber

Chamber of the Great Council
The meeting room for Venice's governing body of aristocrats was huge. It had to be, for the Great Council had more than 1,200 members by 1311.

Bridge of Sighs

Terrible ten
After an attempt to overthrow the Doge in the 14th century, Venetians appointed a council of ten noblemen to make quick decisions. They had great power, and organized a secret service that extended to every possible corner of the known world.

Doge's palace

Unholy trinity
The most feared men in Venice were the three Inquisitors chosen from the Council of Ten. They dealt with matters of state security, and could order the death of almost anyone.

Gondola

Smaller city barge

Doge stands on prow (front) of barge

Gondolas
he hired rowboats of 'enice, called gondolas, re like water taxis.

Dull hull
Vealthy families once ichly decorated their rivate gondolas, but rom 1562 these glitzy oats were outlawed.

Piazzetta

Death in Venice
The Piazzetta in front of the Piazza was the site for the city's public executions. Between the two columns the executioner hanged wrong-doers, or cut their heads off. Bored with humdrum slaughter, he buried three traitors alive here in 1405, leaving only their legs visible.

Bucintoro

Bucintoro
The Doge's barge, *Bucintoro*, was the grandest ship in the Venetian fleet. Once a year, the Doge sailed out into the lagoon on it for a ceremony that symbolized the city's control of the ocean.

Bridge of Sighs
This famous bridge links the Doge's Palace to the office of the Inquisitor. The name comes from the mournful sound that prisoners made as they crossed the canal, for they knew they faced execution or torture.

Tower Bridge

LONDON'S LANDMARK BRIDGE LOOKS LIKE A TALLER TWIN OF THE City's famous Tower nearby. Yet for all the pinnacles and parapets, the castlelike masonry is only skin deep. Under its stone cladding the bridge has a skeleton of steel. Built at the end of the 19th century to relieve traffic congestion, Tower Bridge is a bascule bridge. When a tall ship sails up London's River Thames, the two bascules (leaves that carry the roadway) lift to allow the ship to pass underneath.

Heavy seesaw!
The word *bascule* means "seesaw" in French. On Tower Bridge, lead and steel weights counterbalance the bascules. Each weighs 320 tons (325 tonnes)—as much as 40 African elephants.

Weighty wind
Each bascule, or leaf, weighs 1,200 tons (1,220 tonnes) and is 100 ft (30 m) long. On a still day, little force is needed to lift the bridge. Yet the brid can still open against the strongest gale-force gusts, equivalent to lifting each lea with 150 cars parked on it.

Tower of strength
The original specification for the bridge required that it should be capable of being armed with gu

Original paintwork
Painters covered the metalwork of the bridge with three coats of "bright chocolate" paint before opening day.

Royal opening
The bridge had a royal opening in 1894. Excited crowds gazed as the bridge opened. But not everything went according to plan. Amplified sound was still 20 years in the future, so the royal opening speeches were completely inaudible more than a few feet from the platform.

Chain links
The bridges that link the piers to the banks on either side are suspension bridges; so the supports for the roadway are called "chains," despite the fact that they are really girders.

Dead Man's Hole
An archway under the north approach road gave access to "Dead Man's Hole"—a temporary morgue for bodies fished out of the river close to the bridge.

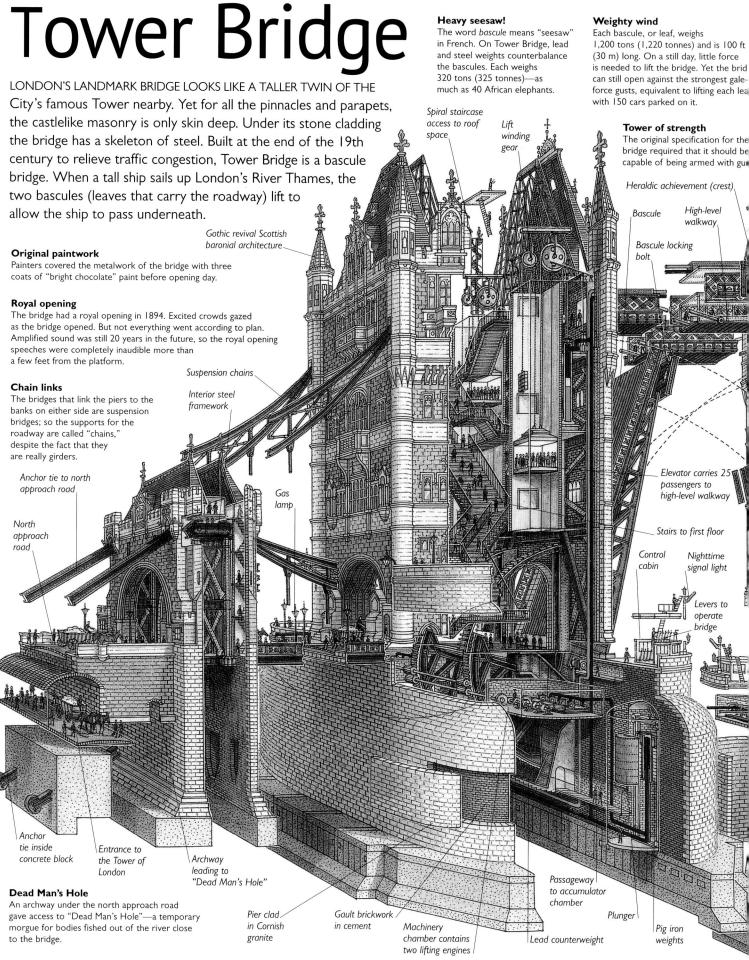

Gothic revival Scottish baronial architecture

Spiral staircase access to roof space

Lift winding gear

Heraldic achievement (crest)

Bascule

High-level walkway

Bascule locking bolt

Suspension chains

Interior steel framework

Anchor tie to north approach road

North approach road

Gas lamp

Elevator carries 25 passengers to high-level walkway

Stairs to first floor

Control cabin

Nighttime signal light

Levers to operate bridge

Anchor tie inside concrete block

Entrance to the Tower of London

Archway leading to "Dead Man's Hole"

Pier clad in Cornish granite

Gault brickwork in cement

Machinery chamber contains two lifting engines

Lead counterweight

Passageway to accumulator chamber

Plunger

Pig iron weights

Bridgemaster's perks
The bridge employed 80 people, 14 on watch at any one time, including a Superintendent Engineer and a Bridgemaster, who had an official residence nearby.

Open wide
The bridge had to provide a very wide opening so that vast square-rigged sailing ships could pass through easily under wind power.

Built on mud
The bridge foundations stand not on bedrock, but on clay. To prevent the bridge from sinking, it rests on huge foundations. The engineers kept the weight down to less than the pressure of someone standing on your toe.

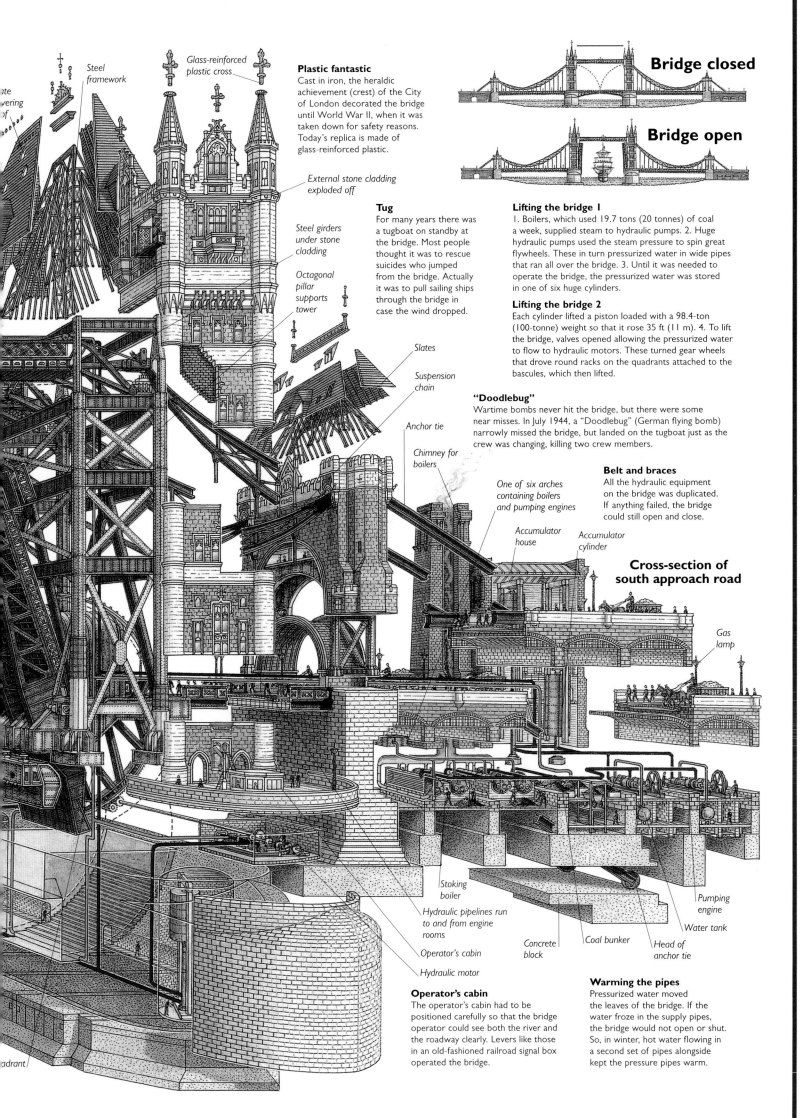

Plastic fantastic
Cast in iron, the heraldic achievement (crest) of the City of London decorated the bridge until World War II, when it was taken down for safety reasons. Today's replica is made of glass-reinforced plastic.

Bridge closed

Bridge open

Steel framework

Glass-reinforced plastic cross

External stone cladding exploded off

Steel girders under stone cladding

Octagonal pillar supports tower

Tug
For many years there was a tugboat on standby at the bridge. Most people thought it was to rescue suicides who jumped from the bridge. Actually it was to pull sailing ships through the bridge in case the wind dropped.

Slates

Suspension chain

Anchor tie

Chimney for boilers

One of six arches containing boilers and pumping engines

Accumulator house

Accumulator cylinder

Lifting the bridge 1
1. Boilers, which used 19.7 tons (20 tonnes) of coal a week, supplied steam to hydraulic pumps. 2. Huge hydraulic pumps used the steam pressure to spin great flywheels. These in turn pressurized water in wide pipes that ran all over the bridge. 3. Until it was needed to operate the bridge, the pressurized water was stored in one of six huge cylinders.

Lifting the bridge 2
Each cylinder lifted a piston loaded with a 98.4-ton (100-tonne) weight so that it rose 35 ft (11 m). 4. To lift the bridge, valves opened allowing the pressurized water to flow to hydraulic motors. These turned gear wheels that drove round racks on the quadrants attached to the bascules, which then lifted.

"Doodlebug"
Wartime bombs never hit the bridge, but there were some near misses. In July 1944, a "Doodlebug" (German flying bomb) narrowly missed the bridge, but landed on the tugboat just as the crew was changing, killing two crew members.

Belt and braces
All the hydraulic equipment on the bridge was duplicated. If anything failed, the bridge could still open and close.

Cross-section of south approach road

Gas lamp

Stoking boiler

Hydraulic pipelines run to and from engine rooms

Operator's cabin

Hydraulic motor

Concrete block

Coal bunker

Head of anchor tie

Pumping engine

Water tank

Operator's cabin
The operator's cabin had to be positioned carefully so that the bridge operator could see both the river and the roadway clearly. Levers like those in an old-fashioned railroad signal box operated the bridge.

Warming the pipes
Pressurized water moved the leaves of the bridge. If the water froze in the supply pipes, the bridge would not open or shut. So, in winter, hot water flowing in a second set of pipes alongside kept the pressure pipes warm.

Human body

A TRIP THROUGH THE HUMAN BODY WOULD BE LIKE SURFING THROUGH THE VAST network of subways and sewers beneath a city. From the pounding heart, you'd slow gradually as the wide tunnels grew narrower and lower, before cruising back to repeat the ride just a minute or so later. A trip around the lungs would be far quicker: sucked down the ribbed trachea, you'd float along increasingly narrow tubes. Just a second later, hurricane-force winds would blow you out again. The brain controls the whole network, sending vital messages sparking through a web of tiny nerves.

Masticating muscle
The masseter muscle enables us to bite and is the body's strongest muscle. Normal bite pressure is about 165–220 lb (75–100 kg), but some people have a bite strength of nearly half a ton.

Reliable ticker
The human heart is an efficient and hard-wearing blood pump. It's only about the size of a fist, yet it can last for 70 years, pumping 30 times its own weight of blood a minute.

Not really bored
The yawn reflex draws air into the lungs when the brain needs more oxygen. This often happens after a long period of inactivity.

Labels (left/lower)

Muscles of chest with veins and arteries covering rib cage

Pleural sac

Trachea (windpipe)

Biceps

Right lung

Heart

Skin and facial hair

Facial muscles

Olfactory nerves in nasal cavity

Olfactory bulb (senses odors)

Pericranium

Lachrimal (tear) gland

Rib cage

Labels (center)

Right cerebral hemisphere

Brain stem

Left cerebral hemisphere

Pia mater (membrane covering brain)

Skull made up of 20 bones

Cerebellum

Liver

Claret of life
Our bodies contain about 1.3 gallons (5 liters) of blood—roughly half a bucketful. Three-fifths of it is coursing through our veins, while at any one moment our lungs contain about two and a half cups of blood. The rest is in the heart, arteries, and capillaries.

Lymphatic system
Another set of vessels in our body is the lymphatic system, which circulates a thin, milky liquid, called lymph. A line of defense and a source of nutrients, lymph contains disease-fighting white blood cells that combat infection. Filters in lymph vessels are known as glands, or nodes. When you are ill, germ-killing cells collect in the nodes to help you fight back.

Gray lump
Despite the awesome power of the brain, it's not much to look at. Some compare the brain's function with a computer's, but the human brain is many millions of times more powerful than even the biggest computers.

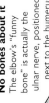

Dura mater (membrane on top of pia mater) absorbs shock

Inner ear

Ear canal

Outer ear

Skin

Hearing bones
Tiny bones in the ear amplify the vibrations of the eardrum to enable us to hear quiet sounds. The stapes, or stirrup bone, is the smallest in the human body. It weighs 0.07–0.15 oz (2–4.3 g), about the same as a sugar cube.

Eustachian tube

Cross-sectioned cervical (neck) vertebrae

Deltoid muscle

Lymph vessels and nodes clustered under armpit

Triceps

No bones about it
The elbow's "funny bone" is actually the ulnar nerve, positioned next to the humerus.

Humerus

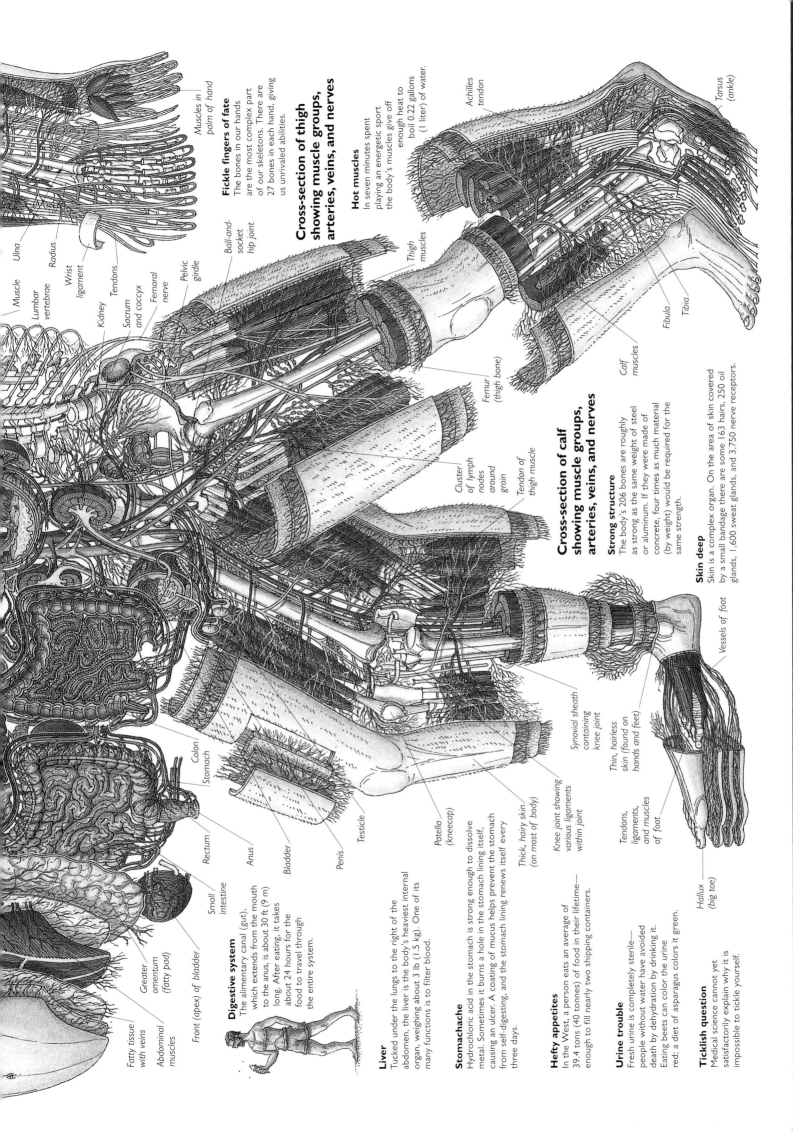

Muscles in palm of hand

Fickle fingers of fate
The bones in our hands are the most complex part of our skeletons. There are 27 bones in each hand, giving us unrivaled abilities.

Cross-section of thigh showing muscle groups, arteries, veins, and nerves

Hot muscles
In seven minutes spent playing an energetic sport the body's muscles give off enough heat to boil 0.22 gallons (1 liter) of water.

Achilles tendon

Ulna

Radius

Muscle

Lumbar vertebrae

Wrist ligament

Kidney

Tendons

Sacrum and coccyx

Femoral nerve

Pelvic girdle

Ball-and-socket hip joint

Thigh muscles

Tibia

Fibula

Calf muscles

Femur (thigh bone)

Cluster of lymph nodes around groin

Tendon of thigh muscle

Cross-section of calf showing muscle groups, arteries, veins, and nerves

Strong structure
The body's 206 bones are roughly as strong as the same weight of steel or aluminum. If they were made of concrete, four times as much material (by weight) would be required for the same strength.

Skin deep
Skin is a complex organ. On the area of skin covered by a small bandage there are some 163 hairs, 250 oil glands, 1,600 sweat glands, and 3,750 nerve receptors.

Vessels of foot

Synovial sheath containing knee joint

Thin, hairless skin (found on hands and feet)

Tendons, ligaments, and muscles of foot

Patella (kneecap)

Knee joint showing various ligaments within joint

Thick, hairy skin (on most of body)

Testicle

Colon

Stomach

Rectum

Anus

Bladder

Penis

Small intestine

Hallux (big toe)

Front (apex) of bladder

Greater omentum (fatty pad)

Fatty tissue with veins

Abdominal muscles

Digestive system
The alimentary canal (gut), which extends from the mouth to the anus, is about 30 ft (9 m) long. After eating, it takes about 24 hours for the food to travel through the entire system.

Liver
Tucked under the lungs to the right of the abdomen, the liver is the body's heaviest internal organ, weighing about 3 lb (1.5 kg). One of its many functions is to filter blood.

Stomachache
Hydrochloric acid in the stomach is strong enough to dissolve metal. Sometimes it burns a hole in the stomach lining itself, causing an ulcer. A coating of mucus helps prevent the stomach from self-digesting, and the stomach lining renews itself every three days.

Hefty appetites
In the West, a person eats an average of 39.4 tons (40 tonnes) of food in their lifetime—enough to fill nearly two shipping containers.

Urine trouble
Fresh urine is completely sterile—people without water have avoided death by dehydration by drinking it. Eating beets can color the urine red; a diet of asparagus colors it green.

Ticklish question
Medical science cannot yet satisfactorily explain why it is impossible to tickle yourself.

Climate zones

Boreal zone
The highest point in the canyon is the North Rim, parts of which are more than 8,140 ft (2,480 m) above sea level. The aspen, fir, and spruce trees are adapted to shed the heavy snows that fall each year.

Underground drainage leads down into canyon

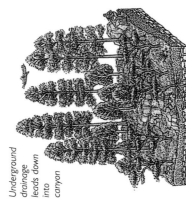

Transition zone
Along the rim in parts of the canyon is the Transition zone. Its climate and wildlife resemble those of both the Upper Sonoran zone above and the Boreal zone below.

Piñon pine

Upper Sonoran zone
The life zone of the upper side of the canyon is called the Upper Sonoran zone. At the top, juniper and piñon

Parking lot

Grand Canyon

EACH YEAR, MORE THAN SIX MILLION PEOPLE FLOCK TO THE southwestern United States to marvel at a vast chunk of emptiness 10 miles (15 km) wide and more than 1 mile (1,500 m) deep. Tourists come to see what the huge gap reveals: a candy-striped fantasy of layered rock. The raging Colorado River created this spectacular gash when it carved its way through the rocks of Arizona, taking five to six million years to complete its work. Just as amazing as the layers of geology are the climate and wildlife of the canyon. The base is a desert where rocks get hot enough to fry eggs in the summer sun. Yet high above on the rim there are pine forests where mountain lions hunt deer in freezing winter snows.

Count 'em
One of the first white men to see the canyon wrote: "Ours has been the first, and will doubtless be the last, party of whites to visit this profitless locality." Now nearly five million tourists visit each year!

Cliffs and slopes
Hard rocks form vertical cliffs; softer rocks weather into steep slopes.

Splat!
Anybody falling from the rim of the canyon would soon strike the sloping sides, but if they had a clear drop to the bottom, they'd have about 35 seconds to admire the view on the way down.

No snow
Snow often dusts the canyon's high North Rim, but it almost never falls to the foot of the canyon.

Crossing the canyon
Trail runners crossing the canyon usually start on the higher and more remote North Rim. The rim-to-rim record for running across is less than 3 hours, but most take 2–4 days.

Hang glider

Exhausted
Some hikers can't complete the climb; the park rangers carry them to the top on mules. These "drag-outs" must pay their fare before getting into the saddle.

Empire State Building

Ocean liner

Winding path leads to bottom

That's deep
The Grand Canyon is deep enough in places to stack four Empire State Buildings, one on top of the other. Its maximum width at the base is equivalent to five ocean liners lined up

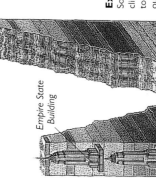

cactus

Lower Sonoran zone
At the bottom of the canyon (and mostly at the western end), the Lower Sonoran zone is a desert environment. Scorpions, more deadly than rattlesnakes, scuttle between the cacti.

Map the gap
The Grand Canyon was one of the last places to be mapped in the US. In 1869, Major John Wesley Powell and nine others traveled the river in boats, and the US Geological Survey produced basic maps in 1902. River maps appeared in 1923.

Desert landscape

Burrowing creature

It's hot down here
The wildlife at the foot of the canyon has adapted to the desert conditions. Many creatures stay in burrows by day, emerging only in the cool of the night.

Rough and smooth
The Colorado River drops about 2,000 ft (600 m) in the canyon: roughly 8 ft each mile (1.5 m/km). However, the descent is not even; some parts are gentle, but in other sections the river flows through ferocious rapids.

Down the river
Riding the river in a wooden rowing boat takes three weeks; the sport began in 1909, and commercial trips started in the 1930s. From the fifties, huge rafts with room for 30 began carrying passengers.

Layers of rock

Waterfall

Helipad

Ancient wonder
The oldest rocks at the foot of the canyon formed about 1,840 million years ago.

manual instructs that "All domestic and grazed animals that die in the park shall be buried immediately."

Rules favor mules
Park rules state that when mules and hikers pass, the quadrupeds pass closest to the canyon side. This can be unnerving for bipeds when the trail is only a little over a mule-belly wide.

widened by blasting out in places, but there are also many steep tracks worn by animals.

Native American granary

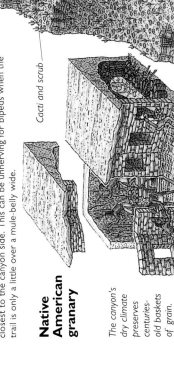

The canyon's dry climate preserves centuries-old baskets of grain.

Cacti and scrub

Canyon dwellers
Native American people explored the canyon perhaps 40 centuries before Europeans first saw it. From about 500 BCE the Anasazi people lived here. They built roomlike grain stores high above the river, often under rock overhangs.

Native American granary

Riverbank

Lush riverbank

Lush riverbanks
In contrast to the desert landscape surrounding it, the riverbank is lush and green.

Darn that dam!
Far more water once flowed down the Colorado, but today Glen Canyon Dam regulates the river flow to generate electricity. When the folks of Phoenix, Las Vegas, and Tucson turn on their air conditioners, engineers at the dam open the sluices and "turn on" the Colorado.

INDEX

ACKNOWLEDGMENTS

Dorling Kindersley would like to thank the following people who helped in the preparation of this book:

Lynn Bresler for the index
Constance Novis for editorial support
Giles Sparrow, Fleur Star, and Bohdan Paraschak
 for research

B.A.A. plc, Heathrow
Jack Fryer and the Cranbrook Windmill Association
Kent Fire Safety Division
Shelter, The National Campaign for
 Homeless People
Shepperton Studios for access to soundstages
 and workshops
Special thanks to:
Lt. Katherine A. McNitt, Station Chief,
National Oceanographic and
Atmospheric Administration,
Amundsen-Scott South Pole Station